BASIC GUIDE TO
MOUNTAIN GARDENING ©

By Antoinette Berthelotte

ACKNOWLEDGEMENTS

I want to thank those many people who helped
me make this book possible and whose
expertise and creativity have enhanced it.

To Margaret Rondeau who has always
encouraged my writing.

To Jan Jasper-Feyer for the cartoons
and to the many members of the Idyllwild
Garden Club who are such avid learners and
teachers!

Published by: Double Fun Press
35061 Barbara Lee Drive
Mountain Center CA 92561
Doublefunpress@yahoo.com – 858-472-4337

Knowing Your Garden

Before you start to plan, or change, your garden, you need to think about any potential challenges you will face. Just like a general before battle, you need to know your terrain, your goals and your options.

Terrain: Terrain encompasses several components, such as:

Physical Features:

When your property consists of slopes, gullies, and rocks etc., it certainly increases the challenges. However, they can also offer a unique and beautiful quality to your garden.

<u>Gullies:</u> Placing stones along a gully can help you direct and control water flow during rainy seasons and protect against excessive erosion. You can create little mini-ponds that don't impede the eventual flow of the water, but slows it by accumulating water in those ponds, thereby giving the water an opportunity to soak into the soil and water plants. It also provides a source of water for our forest creatures.

<u>Rocks:</u> They can create picturesque focal points in a garden. If they have fissures, there are many native plants that love to cling to seemingly soil free rocks. Plants that are sun-shy will do well on the shady sides of rocks and the rocks retain heat from the sun which then radiates and warms plant on cold evenings.

<u>Slopes:</u> If planned properly, slopes can grow gardens almost as easily as a flat surface. Depending on the incline, a simple placement of fencing, horizontal deep raking, or lines of stones, can prevent erosion and lets you plant along the hillside.

If the slope is quite steep, a little digging and stonework can create a terraced garden. This is not only lovely, it is practical. The soil can then be amended as needed with less loss to run-off and terraces make for an easier terrain for walking, watering and weeding. Again, stones absorb sunshine and help radiate heat.

Another option is to sink tubs into the hillside. (See container gardening) This will not change the original run-off pattern of the slope, but they will protect the plants and soil within the containers. By sinking them into the hillside, they will be protected from cold, or moisture loss from heat. This is also the best deterrent against gopher damage.

Soil Types:

Most mountain areas have one or two types of soil. There is decomposed granite (DG) which is low in organic matter. This type also dries out quickly because it often drains water rapidly. It can get quite hot on a summer day yet doesn't retain the sun's heat very well once the coolness of evening comes on. DG doesn't contain much nitrogen, but actually has most other nutrients in its makeup. Keep in mind that since decomposed granite does drain well, this can be a big benefit for many plants who don't like to 'get their feet wet' and who prefer to pull moisture from deep in the earth rather than sit in soggy soil. DG soil also works well for natives as they have already adapted.

The other type of soil contains a lot of clay. This is not as common in the mountains and even though it can be high in nutrients, it is more likely to retain water and has poor drainage. Most plants like some water, but very soggy ground can be death to many of them unless they are commonly found in riparian (natural water sources) settings. Delicate plants can also have a hard time trying to push their stems and roots through dense clay.

Another value you need to consider is the pH value of your soil. What is your native soil? Is it acidic, or alkaline? This is determined by its pH value and is a guide to what will grow well in your soil and if the soil will need amendments to grow what you want. In most mountain environments your soil is going to be less than satisfactory for anything other than what grows naturally in the environment. (I.e. natives)

If you want to plant anything else, it is important to know about the pH of your soil. Different plants require different pH levels, so once you know your soil's pH, you can sow plants that will thrive in that soil, or you can amend the soil to expand the range of plants you can grow.

Getting a measurement is easy, and there are a number of different ways to do it, some of them pretty much free by using household ingredients for the tests.

To determine the pH value and what will be required to change it, you can use one of following methods found on **www.wikihow.com**

Three Methods of Testing Soil pH:

With a Commercial Test Probe:

Use a trowel or spade to dig a hole 2-4 inches deep in the ground. Break up the soil within the hole and remove any twigs or foreign debris.

Fill the hole with water. Use distilled (not spring) water. You can find this in any grocery store. Don't use rainwater as it is slightly acidic and bottled or tap water tends to be slightly alkaline.

Fill the hole until you have a muddy pool at the bottom. Make sure your commercial tester is clean and calibrated (for a more exact measurement). Wipe the probe with a tissue or clean cloth, and insert it into the mud. Hold it there for 60 seconds and take a reading. pH is usually measured on a scale of 1-14, though the tester may not include this entire range. A pH of 7 indicates neutral soil.

A pH above 7 indicates alkaline soil.
A pH below 7 indicates acidic soil.

Take several measurements in different spots in the garden. A single reading may be an anomaly, so it's good to get an idea of the average pH in a plot. If they're all around the same, take the average and amend the soil accordingly. If one spot is very different than the rest, however, you may need to "spot treat" it.

Testing Soil pH Using Red Cabbage:

Take a head of red cabbage and finely chop it using a knife or food processor. Heat distilled water until boiling. Using pure distilled water will give an accurate pH test result.

Add the chopped red cabbage to the boiling distilled water. Allow it to soak for about ten minutes and then drain the solid pieces out, leaving a violet hued juice. This juice should naturally have a neutral pH of about 7. The solution created from the cabbage will then change color depending on the pH of what it comes in contact with.

To test the cabbage juice: Pour a small amount into two separate cups (porcelain or glass) and add vinegar to one cup and baking soda to the other. Vinegar is acidic, and should turn the solution hot pink. The baking soda solution is alkaline and will turn blue or green.

To test your soil: Pour a few inches of the plain cabbage juice into a clean cup and add one to two spoonsful of soil. Wait thirty minutes, and check the color of the solution.

Purple or violet is a pH near 7, neutral.

Pink means the soil is acidic with a pH between 1 and 7. The more acidic the soil is, the brighter the pink will be.

Blue or green is a pH between 8 and 14, alkaline. The brighter green the juice is, the more alkaline it is.

Testing Soil pH Using Vinegar and Baking Soda Only:

Take a cup of debris free soil from your garden. Put a few spoonsful of it into two separate, non-metallic containers. Add vinegar to one container. If it fizzes, it means your soil is alkaline. In that case, you do not need to proceed to the next step. If it doesn't fizz, add water to the other container of soil. You want enough that it becomes very wet and muddy. Pour baking soda into this cup; if it fizzes, it means your soil is acidic. Check both soil samples again. If neither sample began fizzing, it means you probably have a neutral pH of 7. This is good, as this is the pH most plants need to grow in.

Changing Your Soil pH

To make your soil <u>less acidic</u>: If your soil pH tested below 7, add lime or wood ash to the soil. Both are available at local gardening centers.

To make your soil <u>less alkaline</u>: If your soil pH tested above 7, add organic matter such as pine needles, peat moss, or decomposed tree leaves. *(Author's Note: In most cases, mountain soil is more acidic since it naturally has a lot of organic matter in it.)*

Change your soil pH to suit specific plants. For example, add wood ash to a certain area of your garden to encourage the growth of hydrangeas which prefer more alkaline soil. The pH of your soil does not need to be uniform in your entire garden over; feel free to alter it to support different plants.

Amending your Soil:

There are some things to consider regarding amending soil. Other than adjusting the acidity, etc. of the soil, you may want to add other nutrients, especially for edible plants. Soil preparation is often the key to growing healthy plants in the mountains, particularly for non-native plants. In fact, it is not a good idea to amend soil for natives since they are already adapted to your natural soil. You may well find that the native plants do flourish at first, in amended soil, but will have a much shorter life span.

Mulch: Organic mulch, such as bark, leaves, pine needles, etc. not only adds nutrients, it keeps weeds at bay, retains moisture, improves the soil, reduces erosion, insulates root systems and helps a garden look well maintained.

Fertilizers vs Nutrients:

You'll have access to multiple types of commercial fertilizers that can be added to your soils in several ways. However, the key to a truly healthy garden is the soil itself. In each handful of soil there are billions of invisible organisms. Some are harmful, but many are of such importance that life on earth would cease to exist without them! Therefore, the relationship between the nutrients we add, and the soil itself, is quite symbiotic. For example, when we add a fertilizer to a garden, very little of it is absorbed by the roots of the plants! What we just added and the roots are but a small percentage of the soil. However, the existing organisms absorb most of those added nutrients and use them for their own growth. The good news is that these organisms have short life spans and when they die, they release more of those nutrients. In this way, the nutrients are released to the roots over a prolonged period of time. The more organic materials we can instill into the soil, the better, whether it is in the form of compost, tilled plant life, well-rotted manure, etc. Even tilling the soil can be a benefit since so much of our natural topsoil has been removed through construction and clearing.

Year after year of such loving treatment to our soil creates that lovely word 'loam'. Loam is easy to work, rich, drains well and grows wonderful crops.

How much amendment you add depends on how well the soil drains. If it doesn't drain well, don't add a lot at once. Add a little each year so that the salts and chemicals don't build up to a high level. Incorporate 2 to 3 inches of organic matter (or 3 cubic yards per 1,000 square feet of garden), such as alfalfa pellets, compost, or aged manure, to a depth of 6 to 12 inches. It is best to work organic matter into the entire area that will be planted. Basically, dig a hole more than 6 to 12 inches deep, piling the dirt to one side. Add amendments of about 20% of the volume removed, and incorporate it into the pile of dirt you dug. Now you can refill your garden area with that amended soil. You want to make it well mixed and deep so you don't create an amended layer of a just few inches over the plain natural soil. The plants will probably do well for a short period of time, but once the roots grow through that thin layer, they will run into the un-amended soil and the different density, when it may stop growing well.

Topography:

This means the lay of the land. Is your property hilly, rocky, flat, or full of trees? Does it contain streambeds or swampy area?   Being a successful gardener depends on your knowledge of your property.

       Some plants miraculously thrive growing in the crevices of shaded of rocks. Other plants, such as tomatoes absolutely won't! Some plants require deep soft dirt in which to sink their roots, others prefer to send their roots outward and only an inch or two under the surface. Some plants like to have moistness nearby; others will die from the loving gardener drowning them with overwatering.

       Speaking of moisture, observe the flow of runoff during heavy rains. You won't want a garden where 'A River Runs Through It! Also determine if water has a tendency to sit on the surface, runs-off and does not absorb properly. If the soil is so dense that it is unable to absorb, it will need to be improved to a depth of 2 to 3 feet to enhance its absorption rate.

       You should also determine north, south east, west, and track where and for how long the sun shines during the growing seasons. A shady corner in the winter may receive a generous amount of sunshine in the summer! If a plant requires eight or more hours of sunshine, it won't do well if it is in shade for half the day. If you have a lot of shade creating obstacles, you may have to plan multiple small plots rather than one large garden. Also consider exposure to high winds that can flatten plants, or rip away at delicate blossoms. Steep slopes can create disastrous runoff problems. There are solutions to these problems, such as wind-breaks and terracing.

If you already have large bushes and trees, remember that they are drawing nutrients from the soil around them. Therefore, give them some space and don't plant anything that will be competing for water and nutrients or both will suffer.

Weather and Sunlight:

There is no doubt that gardening in the mountains can be challenging, particularly above 5,000'. Most mountains have a number of micro-climates depending on the lay of the land, elevation, shade and exposure. Of course highly forested areas give limited garden spots and will stay colder longer than open areas. When there is direct sunlight it is usually of high intensity and can damage cool weather plants quickly.

Most mountains have low humidity and cold air has a drying effect. Put a slice of bread in the refrigerator and see how quickly it dries out! Combinations of cool nights, a short growing season, drying winds, steepness of slopes, aspect, topography, and soil all influence how well plants perform in these climates. However, most of these challenges can be overcome with proper site preparation and plant choice. Often simply moving a less than robust plant to a new location may help it thrive.

Which plants will put up with lower light levels? A general rule is that plants grown for their stems, leaves or buds generally tolerate light shade fairly well. Those grown for roots or fruits tend to need more sun. That said, those commonly sun loving plants will also tolerate light shade, simply providing smaller yields. They are the ones marked with an asterisk (*)

The following will grow with as little as three to six hours of sun per day, or constant dappled shade. While size or yields may be affected, the taste will be just as good.

Lettuce	Pak Choy
Arugula	Beets *
Spinach	Kohlrabi *
Broccoli *	Brussels Sprouts
Green onions	Mustard greens
Cabbage *	Thyme
Parsley	Coriander
Sorrel	Tarragon
Garlic	Radishes
Cardamom	Potatoes *
Rhubarb *	Swiss Chard

Kale

Carrots *

Gooseberries

Dill

Strawberries *

Blackberries, etc. *

Mint

Collards

Endive

Cress

Cauliflower *

Peas *

Currants

Turnips *

Sweet potatoes and yams *

Cilantro

Lemon Balm

Beans *

Keep in mind:

If trees or other large plants are the source of shade, garden plants may not only have to compete for light but also nutrients and water.

The amount of shade may vary by the seasons when the angle of the sun is different. Study your land carefully and see if sunlight is a bigger or smaller problem than you may have thought later in the season.

Bright and light surfaces nearby (such as white fences or walls) can increase the amount of light plants get.

Morning shade and afternoon shade differ in their effects on garden plants. Some cool season vegetables may actually prefer lots of morning sun and then shade during the hot summer afternoons.

Areas with partial shade in the afternoon can also extend the growing season for some cool season crops that are prone to bolting during higher heat, such as lettuce.

Pay attention to air circulation. Walls and branches can block air flow, allowing moisture to build up and encourage some diseases. Plant crops with more space between them in shady areas, and be careful to water around the root area and not soak leaves from above.

Pruning nearby trees and bushes can dramatically help increase sun exposure.

It's even more important to keep weeds at bay for shade crops that are already competing for light, water and nutrients in less ideal conditions.

Your Game Plan:

If you haven't done so already, this is where you should start sketching out your garden. Depending on your available space, you may have a vegetable garden, a lush flower garden, a native plant garden, an herb garden, a container garden, or all of the above!

Don't forget to think about any limitations you may have when making these plans. These may be personal physical limitations, but also how much time you will have to work in your garden, what tools you have on hand, or need to buy, if your area is in a serious drought etc. Last, but not least, consider your level of experience! If you are a novice, or have never gardened in your current climate, you may be spending time and money that could be wasted and frustrating. Smaller is better at first. A novice usually doesn't realize how time consuming preparation, weeding, dead-heading, watering, and pruning can be. However, if the garden you plant is small enough to be manageable, those activities can be very satisfying and enjoyable.

Also, consider whether your garden will not be tended for days, or weeks, at a time. If so, you will be pretty much limited to natives and other drought resistant plants, unless you have a watering/irrigation system installed with a timer. If not, make sure they have enough water to get established when first planted. A medium amount of water once a week for a month, or two should do it. If you are fairly sure of sufficient spring, or fall rains, after planting, this may take care of that issue. If you do have some plants that will require more frequent watering and they are in a small area, you may be able to find a kind neighbor to help you out.

Vegetable gardens and many flowering plants are thirsty and more labor intensive. Be sure you have them near a ready source of water. You do not want to be schlepping watering cans back and forth! Gardening is supposed to be enjoyable. Of these two choices, vegetable gardens are the more challenging; however, they can be most rewarding. Picture stepping into your backyard and picking everything you need for your dinner salad, fresh, tasty and insecticide free!

You might also want to plant shade friendly flowers around your house because, even on very chilly nights, the radiated warmth from the house prolongs their growth and blossoms by almost an extra month in the spring and again in the fall.

A word about chilly nights; talk to locals about when to plant. It's difficult to see all of the nurseries full of plants and packets of seeds, in early spring and to feel the warmth of an exceptionally balmy April and not want to plant NOW! But Mother Nature has a wicked sense of humor and will insist you wait. The first year in my mountain home, I planted tomatoes three times in a row and watched them freeze before it was finally the right time. Don't even think about anything but soil preparation before mid-May. If you want crops that require longer growing seasons, start your seeds indoors, or in a greenhouse.

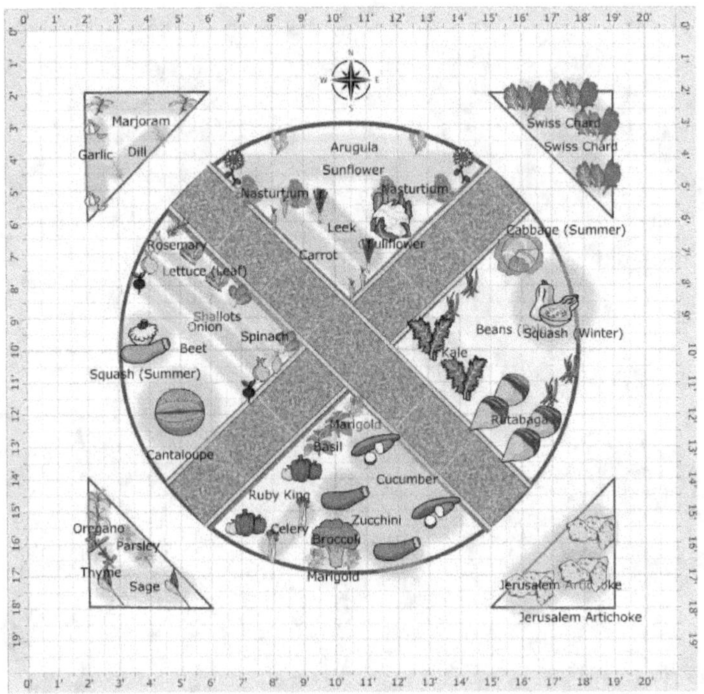

For <u>small gardens</u> you might simply prefer to buy plants that are already potted and growing and keep them protected and where they can get some sun, until frost danger is past. However, don't try to keep them in those little pots for more than four weeks, or they won't be as healthy as they should be for transplanting. Buying those plants is definitely the easiest and surest way to get a good crop a bit earlier.

Critter Control

Varmint Invasions:

Discouraging Gophers, Moles, Voles, Deer, Ground and Tree squirrels, Raccoons, Mice, Ants, Rabbits, etc. from using your garden as their local buffet takes patience and a willingness to experiment with several tactics to find the one that works best.

You will find many of the following suggestions to be easy and not terribly expensive solutions. We hope you will try some of the more humane options first and only resort to the more 'permanent' when necessary. After all, we need these little beasts to balance our ecosystem and many of them give us much pleasure on a daily basis. Let me preface the following with the fact that there are no <u>guaranteed</u> varmint resistant plants, or methods. If animals are hungry enough, they will eat anything! Just saying!

Let's take a few minutes to discuss the three major ways to deal with wildlife that is invading your garden. They are extermination (a socially acceptable word for killing), repelling and protection.

Extermination:

There have been many a gardener who, upon seeing his time, efforts and money go for naught, would gladly go on a rampage and kill any hapless creature in the vicinity. However, extermination has its own drawbacks, over and beyond moral grounds. If an animal is killed, there are many more to just move in and take over. It may slow down the breeding process, but not by much and certainly not enough to save your garden. It is also cruel to kill one who may have babies somewhere, thereby condemning them to a slow, cruel, death by starvation. I have also seen gardeners killing animals who were not the culprits. So, think first before you choose to kill. Unless it's Godzilla. If it's Godzilla, go ahead and kill him!

Repel and Protect:

What we are hoping you will do is to try to repel your furry visitors, or protect your garden from them. You can often repel with sounds, scents, or grow plants that are the animal's last choice to eat. Protection is often your best bet if done well. It's better to prevent than to try to cure.

Wildlife needs food too and you can't blame them for finding the easiest and juiciest morsels available. If they cannot get to your plants, they will go forth and forage and all of you can live in harmony.

By the way, we do not recommend using netting, such as bird netting, especially at ground level. A large number of birds and animals can get trapped and tangled. I doubt you would want to rescue a skunk from such a situation, nor would you want to let an animal die trapped like that.

The following suggestions try to incorporate each of these options, with the protection option often being inferred. Be sure to also read the chapter about container and containment gardening.

Some Basics:

Just because you see rabbits, or squirrels, or raccoons, it doesn't mean you have to take action. I have a family of rabbits that visit my yard, eat some of my grass and have yet to bother my garden! I simply leave them alone and enjoy watching them. Our grey squirrels do little damage and the trade- off of watching their antics is worth it. If, however, they start to cause problems, refer to the appropriate section in this book.

Something else to consider is being sure to avoid handling wildlife. You shouldn't have to, but sometimes we accidentally 'corner' an animal. When frightened, any animal will panic and may well try to defend itself. You will usually end up worse for wear in this encounter. If you have any possibility of coming in close proximity to wildlife, especially around traps, wear long thick gloves and protective clothing. If you find an injured or sick animal, contact your local wildlife rehabilitation center.

To prevent 'inviting' wildlife into your home and garden follow some of these guidelines:

Let wildlife find its own food in nature. Do not intentionally feed wildlife or unintentionally leave food available in open garbage cans, open compost piles, and pet food dishes. A bungee cord across can lids is often a sufficient deterrent. Pick up fallen fruits and nuts.

Feeding wild birds can be a problem. Birds will become dependent on you, and spilled seed will attract unwanted critters. If you still want to have a bird feeder, try to keep it away from the garden, your house, or any outbuildings used for storage. However, birdbaths filled with fresh water daily are good for birds all year long.

Close all access holes in your home. Typically, holes occur in foundation vent screens, under the eaves, in the roof, in the sub-floor, in closets, and under doors. Such openings are like invitations that say, "Welcome, please come in" to critters who are searching for shelter and food. Use inexpensive hardware cloth to close the openings. Capping your chimney with a spark arrester not only protects against fire, it also closes a possible way into your home.

Hardware cloth is made from galvanized metal or stainless steel. Stainless steel is more expensive but long-lasting, as it will not rust. It comes in 1, 2, 3 or 4 mesh or <u>squares </u>per inch. The 1/4-inch mesh is more flexible than the larger mesh patterns.

The larger mesh product is a sturdy fence material. Gopher wire, on the other hand is hexagonal like chicken wire, but with smaller gaps. It is made of a lighter gauge metal, which makes it flexible enough to shape into cages that will fit around roots of vegetables, etc.

If you find that a wild critter has accidentally entered your residence, close the interior doors to the room where it is, and open windows and doors leading outside. Stay out of sight to avoid frightening the critter. The animal will usually exit on its own. When it does, shut the windows and doors. *(This method seldom works with mice unless you can chase them out with a broom, etc.!)*

Ants in your Plants (and House):

Ants outside are not really pests. They are great for cleaning up nature's trash and enriching the soil with organic compounds. If you see ants crawling on your plants, don't panic. They are not likely to do any damage and may well be fulfilling part of the pollination function as they drag pollen from one spot to another. If they are crawling into your hummingbird feeders etc. you can use something like Vaseline on the support wire or post to prevent access.

However, even though it doesn't involve your garden, I am going to address ants in your home. Going to the kitchen in the morning to see a countertop covered with ants is not a good way to start your day. Ants are basically harmless, even those who find their way into your home. Fortunately they are fairly easy to discourage. Be sure you try the following before using more draconian measures, such as pesticides

First, remove whatever attracts them. There are ants that are attracted to sweets, proteins (meat, raw eggs, and grease) or can simply be seeking moisture and coolness. Watch where they come from and note what area or foodstuffs around which they are congregating. Here's a clue. If you have a sugar bowl full of ants, they are..... wait for it..... Sugar ants!

Once the food source is gone, the ants will go elsewhere to seek sustenance. Keep your kitchen and house clean. Do not leave crumbs, garbage, or food accessible. Thoroughly clean up grease and spills. Keep sweet foods in containers that have been washed to remove residues on outer surfaces. Rinse out empty soft drink containers and remove them from the building. Feed pets indoors; then seal and put away leftover pet food.

If you simply see a few random ants, they are scouts and will go back to headquarters to report a lack of food at your address. Even if this is the case, try to discover the ant's trail in your house. Follow these hints as a way to discourage and get rid of them.

Find their point of entry and find what is attracting them.

Remove the lure and without killing any ants, completely clean the area where the food source was. If you kill the ants, it attracts others to come in to remove their dead and you just have more ants!

As difficult as it might be, do the above and wait up to 24 hours and the ants will exit where they entered if you haven't left anything else to attract them.

If they are not all gone overnight, with a *soft* brush you can *gently* sweep any remaining ants into a dustpan and deposit them outdoors without injuring them.

After they have left, plug, or seal, the opening they used to come in.

Be sure to use soapy water, or vinegar and water, to wipe over the path they used. They're like little scouts, carefully leaving a scent trail for their friends to follow.

Place a piece of plastic wrap or paper with the following deterrents: drops of peppermint oil, chopped fresh mint, sliced garlic cloves, fresh cloves, shredded lemon peel or a product called Orange Guard, at the place where the ants entered. Use any one of these repellents or a combination of them.

You really shouldn't need to use pesticides. It is to your benefit not too since ants are usually in the kitchen and laying down toxic powders, or spray, endangers you too.

Dealing With Deer:

Most mountain gardeners are in a love/hate relationship with deer. They probably love seeing these graceful and beautiful animals around their home. However, if they are destroying your garden it leaves you no choice but to take some action. The first thing you need to do to co-exist is to try to use plants that are on the deer's do-not-eat list. Simply look up 'Deer Resistant Plants' on the Internet, use the Sunset Western Gardening book, or check with your local garden club since the plants will vary depending upon your geographical location. Keep in mind that these plants are not their favorite, but if hungry, will do in a pinch. There is a consensus that deer especially dislike plants in the mint and lavender family.
If your garden consists of vegetation that attracts deer and deer are around, you can expect them to show up and enjoy. NOTE: The most active browse times for deer are early morning, dusk into evening, and moonlit nights.

You can try repellants if the deer's visits are random and it doesn't seem they've got you on their 'go to' list.

<u>Some suggestions are:</u>

Human hair: Easy enough to get a lot just by collecting some at the local barber or beauty salon. Just scatter in your garden on a regular basis.

Spray the deer's favorites with hot pepper spray.

Plant what they don't like. For example: They do not like ornamental grasses, **iris**es, foxglove, yucca, herbs and plants with a strong fragrance, such as sage, **chives**, lemon balm, bee balm, etc. They also dislike plants with thorns, such as purple coneflower. Unfortunately, roses seem to be a big exception to that!

Commercial and home-made deer repellent are an option. These can be purchased from garden or hardware stores. Use these products according to their instructions. With very little trouble, you can make your own for a lot less money! Using a loosely woven bag, like onions come in; hang them from low branches, deer height, around the garden. Place decaying fish heads, blood, bone meals, garlic, fabric softener, animal urine or mothballs. Mothballs smell better to us, but do contain many chemicals.

Repellents need to be applied monthly, unless there is a lot of rain, then applies when the weather clears up. Don't forget to apply it to new growth as needed. The Humane Society of the United States advises that repellents with putrid odors such as the sulphur-based odor of rotten eggs seem to be more successful than taste-based repellents. The drawback to deer repellants is that they, well, stink. They may take away from the ambience of your garden. However, soap flakes scattered around the perimeter of your garden may discourage the deer.

You can also try motion sensor lights, shiny objects like foil and/or shiny CDs tied about deer height, or something that triggers noise to scare them away.

If all else fails and you are losing the battle due to deer, you're going to have to build fences, or enclosures specifically designed for deer. The good news is they will keep most other above ground critters away.

You will need a polypropylene mesh, woven wire or solid wood fence at least 8-10 feet high. The longevity of a good fence makes it a good investment. Many gardeners actually sink an extra 6, or 12 inches of fencing below the surface since fawns, and other small critters, are very adept at crawling under fences. Be sure any openings are too small for any animal to gain access, or in which they could get stuck, leaving them to suffer. Putting a surrounding lower layer of wire mesh fencing will avoid that problem. Don't use any protuberances, such as pointed ends, that could impale, or injure, a deer trying to clear a fence. Deer don't have the capacity to recognize that as a danger so it won't discourage them.

A fairly new, novel idea is using Irish Spring Soap. Sure smells better to us than some of the other suggestions, but the deer don't like it. Leave the box and/or wrapper on and drill a hole through the centers. Thread a string, or wire, through the hole in each bar. Then hang each individual string with its bar of soap on bushes and trees 3 feet apart up to a height of 6'. You can also shred Irish Spring Soap and scatter it throughout your garden.

"Get!" Gophers:

As hard as it is to believe, gophers can be beneficial to our environment! When not visiting yards and gardens they are busy tilling and improving soil with their insistent digging. They are also a food source for many of nature's animals and raptors. However, they can also quietly and quickly decimate a garden.

The commonly known Pocket Gopher, so

named for their external pouched cheeks, have been with us for eons so we shouldn't be surprised that they are difficult to get rid of. They are about the size of prairie dogs and have stocky, furred bodies, short legs and tails, strong, almost talon-like claws, and long chisel-like teeth that can get through even the toughest dirt. You can identify a gopher mound by the way the dirt mound is thrown out in a fan-shaped with a plugged hole in the "handle" of the fan. Gophers have a good sense of touch and smell and eat about 75% of their body weight daily in the form of roots of grasses and plants, vegetables, dandelions and other weeds. Gophers produce small litters of three to four, from January through April, during their 3 year life span.

Other than very brief moments while tunneling to the surface, or when the young leave the burrow to find a new location, they are never above ground. Their natural predators, raccoons, snakes, coyotes, owls, hawks and domestics, such as cats and dogs, are more adept at catching them during those brief forays than man. We will address poisons later, but if for no other reason, it is best to avoid indiscriminately dispersing poisons since other animals, including your pets, may eat the poison, or by eating a poisoned gopher, other animals will also ingest the poison. The same thing goes for above ground lethal traps which are also a danger to children.
Those mini-Hemingways who relish the hunt and feeling of power when catching and killing a gopher need to keep one thing in mind; these persistent ground dwellers can reproduce at a rate that will increase their population within six months, with little effect on diminishing the destruction of the garden.

What is needed to truly make progress is to discourage them from choosing your garden as a home. There are several modes of getting the gophers to move on, and using a combination of these should do the trick.

<u>Stinky Stuff!</u> A Gopher's sense of smell is excellent and they are very sensitive to smells. The best way to give him a whiff of something repulsive is to find the gopher's lateral tunnel. Do this by using a stick to find the 1-1/2" plug in the "handle" of the fan-shaped gopher mound. Poke around the perimeter to search for the entrance to the lateral tunnel that leads down to the gopher's main tunnel a foot below ground level. Insert foul-smelling repellents such as used cat litter or a rag soaked with human urine into a tin can with both ends removed. Place the can in the lateral passageway. Usually within a day or two, you will see another gopher mound quite close to the original. Repeat the process at each new site. He will soon assume he's in a very bad neighborhood and move on to seek more pleasant surroundings. Unless you are looking for a full time job, your main goal should be to just chase them away from your plants, not to eradicate all of the gophers on your block!

Another option is the use of castor oil. Be sure you buy the kind intended for garden use. Wet the ground in areas you wish to protect with a castor oil/water mixture by attaching a container of castor oil to a hose-powered sprayer. Most garden stores offer several castor oil-based gopher and mole repellents that do not harm plants. Keep in mind that you will also notice an odor, but it shouldn't be overpowering.

<u>Protection:</u> Using a wire cage (s) is the most common protection in areas with gopher problems. Just think of it as putting in a fence underground! These special "gopher-proof baskets and root guards" are made of strong galvanized hexagonal steel mesh that gophers cannot chew through. They can be purchased in various sizes, depending on the size of the plant's roots, or can be made by you out of rolls of 'gopher wire'. Even though they look similar, don't use chicken wire. The hexagonal openings are too large. This wiring protects the critically important root crown from which the other roots grow. For larger areas, rather than one cage per individual plant, dig out a larger area and line the bottom and sides with the gopher wire. If there are overlaps, interweave the edges so the gophers don't squeeze over one edge and under the other. No matter which type you use, be sure the top edges are at, or above, the top layer of soil. The gophers won't come up and climb over the top, but if the top in underground at all; they will get into your garden. The premade cages and gopher wire can be found at nurseries, hardware/garden stores, and online.

Just as above ground fences protect your garden from deer, Over/Under fencing of a specific area for ornamentals or vegetables is a reliable way to keep gophers out of that specific area. Install 1/2" inch metal hardware cloth to a depth of at least 2-3 feet below grade and extend about 6-8 inches above grade around the perimeter of the area to be protected. Most gopher's tunnel are about a foot underground, so 2 to 3 feet underground will prevent most, if not all invasions. You will want to allow enough depth and openings to allow root growth out of harm's way.   Certainly one of the benefits of these types of protection is that it is permanent if installed properly and maintained.

After the fencing etc. is up, you may find a gopher was inadvertently fenced in! You may want to deal with this by trapping it. If you use a humane trap such as Havahart Trap be sure you release the gopher on your property. In most states, it is illegal to release a rodent in the wild, or on someone else's property. If you do trap a live gopher, do not touch it or be in such proximity that you could be bitten.
Plant daffodils around your garden. Daffodils repel gophers.

Use nature's own defenses by having some gopher snakes taking care of business. If you haven't any owls in your area, look up what kind is native to your area and build an appropriate owl box in trees nearby. Keep in mind that owls will also eat other small furry creatures, including tiny dogs or cats. Just a word to the wise!

Oddly enough, if you leave one area in, or just outside of, your garden to go to weed, you may lessen the gopher problem. It seems weeds are a favorite food of gophers. You may find that gophers take up residence in that one section and dine on the weeds, leaving the rest of the garden almost entirely alone.

If you haven't protected your garden don't plant in gopher-friendly rows. Gophers like a long row of plants that is easy to follow. A gopher's idea of a produce aisle!

<u>Repelling:</u> Gophers don't like vibrations, or ultra-high frequencies. In a breezy area the vibration from a windmill- like fan may disturb gophers. The "Mole [and gopher] Chaser" is one example of a windmill. The sound of the wind passing over soda pop bottles set partly into the ground is also said to disturb both gophers and rabbits. There are several brands of solar and battery-run sonic devices that can be placed at intervals around your garden.

<u>Poisons:</u> The only poison we will address is using a special tool to introduce the poison directly into the gopher's tunnel system. This is because it is the only way one can be fairly sure the poison will not be accessible to other animals. The gopher/mole stick is a long tube with a small, closable, hole at the pointed end and a handle with a pellet container and release mechanism. A common brand is the Yard Butler.

Each time a mound is found, use the pointed end of the stick to prod around the opening (not in the center of it) to find a tunnel. There will be a sudden lack of pressure, or friction that will indicate the stick has entered the tunnel. The user then uses the release mechanism which opens the hole at the bottom of stick, thereby releasing the poisoned pellets directly into the tunnel. Since this creates little disturbance, the gopher is less likely to simply backfill the tunnel. The gopher(s) will find and consume the pellets, taking some back to their burrow to share with the others. Seldom do gophers come to the surface. They usually die in the ground which prevents predators from eating them and ingesting the poison also. Within 3 days, there should be no more signs of activity around that mound.

The Speedy Ground Squirrel:

The common California Ground Squirrel is found in the northern part of Baja California, throughout California, western Oregon, and central Washington. The squirrel measures between 16 to 18 inches in length, including its bushy tail that is about five to seven inches long. A larger ground squirrel, the Rock Squirrel, is found in southern Nevada, Utah, Colorado, Arizona, New Mexico, western Texas, and the panhandle of Oklahoma. Ground squirrels den underground. They can climb, too. These fascinating and adept small mammals are found in agricultural and rural areas as well as in vacant lots and gardens in populated areas. They tend to avoid areas that are very moist. If they are not causing any significant damage, just sit back and enjoy them, that is, when they slow down enough to watch!

If you are having problems with them here are some ways to deter them.

Don't feed them. Don't feed ground squirrels or any wild animal. They have evolved to find their own food. If wild animals are fed by humans they will stay around and their population will likely increase. They will also learn to depend on humans to provide for them. They love to dine under birdfeeders where there is usually a nice layer of easily accessible seeds.

Therefore, remove attractants; modify their habitat to encourage them to move elsewhere. Remove old pipes, rock piles, brush piles, and debris among which they like to scamper.

Let weeds, grasses, and other vegetation grow high. They don't like tall vegetation because it prevents them from seeing approaching predators.

Wrap sheet metal cylinders around fruit and nut trees to prevent easy climbing. Install solid fences to limit ground squirrels' ability to see their predators. They will feel less safe.

Provide mounds for them. Give them a place to go. Ground squirrels are attracted to gently raised mounds of earth and rocks. If you have enough space on your property, consider attracting them to elevated mounds in a specific area. Then erect a solid fence of wood or shade cloth with tall vegetation next to it to make a visual barrier between the area with the mounds and the rest of your property.

Repellents: Spray **Ropel** on ornamental <u>plants that humans don't eat.</u> Ropel makes the plants taste bitter to the squirrels.

Try some of those **deterrents** we suggested for gophers.
You can also make the ground uncomfortable for them. They like soft dry soil, so making it wet is a deterrent. Ground squirrels eat lawn grass, leaves, seeds, and insects so it's tough to get rid of all their food. If you can at least keep the food they like to a minimum, the population should stay steady. As with most natural strategies, expect that it will take time for these methods to produce results. Eventually you'll achieve a level of harmonious co-existence.

Mother the Mole – Vanquish the Vole:

Moles are NOT rodents. They don't eat plants. In fact, they are often called "the gardener's best friend" because they aerate the soil and consume pesky insects and grubs. Moles are insectivores that feed day and night, ridding the lawn and garden of grubs, slugs, slug eggs, beetles, moth larvae, earwigs, snails, and sow bugs. Only occasionally do they eat a little vegetation. If something is nibbling your plants it could be voles, who sometimes borrow mole tunnels. However, if you do have a heavy infestation of moles, they can inadvertently do some serious damage by undermining your garden area. In that case, refer to actions taken against Gophers.

Moles have heavyset bodies, 4" to 6" long, short legs with five fingered "hands," and eyes that are almost blind. They spend almost all of their time underground in tunnels, using feeding tunnels near

the surface, and deeper, permanent tunnels up to 30" below ground.

Tunnels near the surface appear as narrow strips of slightly raised earth and mole hills. A mole arranges its excavated earth in small circular hills (molehills) with a plugged hole in the middle. In contrast, gophers push the earth into fan-shaped mounds with the entrance hole at one side.

Moles are highly territorial and do not tolerate overlap with other moles. Therefore, if you have evidence of mole activity, probably just one active mole is there, patrolling its tunnels for grubs and insects.

Your grass may be greener and stronger in areas where a mole is active due to the moles beneficial aeration and grub removal services. Because of all their assistance in soil aeration and pest control, one gardening blog states, "The best way to control moles is to do nothing at all. Live peacefully with them." One gardener has written, "A single, resident mole is a welcome tenant."

Moles rarely come to the surface, but if they do and you find yourself in close proximity, be cautious; they do bite! If you have a mole in your garden, simply leave it alone. Tamp down the slightly raised tunnels near the surface and smooth out molehills with a rake.

Regarding Voles: These can become a problem. If you see 1 to 2-inch pathways through grassy areas that are sprinkled with clippings and droppings, and the pathways end at 2- inch-wide, open burrows, you may have voles in your garden. Voles are commonly called meadow mice. The most easily identifiable sign of this type of vole is its extensive surface runway system with multiple burrow openings to the voles' underground nests of grass, stems, and leaves. Overhanging vegetation often obscures their runways. In some areas, voles can exhibit a variety of colors—brown, gray, and even some red, and most have gray under parts. They measure about 5"to 7" in length, nose to tip of their short tail (which is less than 3 inches long), and have stocky bodies and short legs. Voles tend to be less shy than gophers and moles and can sometimes be seen searching for food in the open.

They do not hibernate. If they are lucky enough to elude their natural predators (coyotes, snakes, hawks, and owls as well as humans) they may live out their short natural life of 12-14 months. It is important to remember that vole populations are cyclical. Their population fluctuates unpredictably from year to year, with peak populations occurring every 2 to 5 years. A bumper crop this year may be followed by a much smaller number of voles the following year.

Voles spend the majority of their time searching for food such as grasses, vegetables, and grain crops. Sometimes their gnawing may girdle and endanger young trees. Their gnaw marks on tree trunks tend to be irregular and at various angles, 1/8-inch wide by 3/8-inch long and 1/16-inch or more deep, smaller than the gnaw marks of rabbits.

Killing voles by trapping is a temporary measure at best. If often leads to repopulation of the property by other voles who take advantage of the newly available ecological niches left by the voles that were killed. Using poisons and traps is inhumane and can harm children, pets, and other wildlife. Poisons also travel up the food chain. There are much better ways to discourage voles.

A garden with plentiful weeds, ground cover, heavy mulch, un-mowed lawn, and unmanaged areas with dense vegetation under which to hide becomes a vole-friendly habitat. Push excessive mulch 3 feet away from trees; clear out tall weeds adjacent to gardens; and keep lawns mowed. Tilling the soil can discourage voles by removing cover for their runways and burrow openings.

Grow plants such as daffodils that are less attractive to voles than preferred plants, such as tulips.

Weed-free buffer zones as much as 10 feet wide around areas requiring protection make it difficult for voles to cross the open strip into the garden. Their safety is jeopardized when they can be seen in the open.

If voles are gnawing on saplings, 1/4-inch mesh or hardware cloth can be wrapped around tree trunks and buried about 6-8 inches deep in the ground around the trunks. The same size hardware cloth can be laid on the ground after planting vegetable and flower seeds. As the plants grow through the mesh the voles will be blocked from reaching roots and tubers.

Protect flower bulbs by soaking them in repellents, such as Shotgun Deer and Rabbit Repellent, which contain thiram, a bittering agent. If you use a repellent on a food crop, make sure that the label says it is safe to use on food crops.

Other repellents such as **Ropel**, Plantskyyd, and hot pepper sauce can be applied according to the label's directions. They will need to be re-applied periodically.

Course materials such as diatomaceous earth and coarse gravel, dug into the soil around a flower bed or sprinkled on vole runs, is abrasive to voles touch, encouraging them to leave. One garden advisor recommends sprinkling diatomaceous earth and Bon Ami cleansing powder around trees and shrubs, and applying it in combination with lawn food. He suggests sprinkling Bon Ami alone into planting holes.

Many larger mammals and birds prey upon voles. Hawks and owls are major predators of voles.

Use traps only as last resort—try everything else first. Humane Havahart traps baited with a mix of oatmeal or peanut butter can catch voles alive. Release them unharmed, without touching them, on your own property in a shrubby area away from your protected garden area. Be careful and gentle with them, as they will need to be in good condition when starting their new life away from your favorite garden area. Live traps can also catch other wildlife that you will then need to release. Therefore, live traps should only be used as a last resort.

Glued/Sticky traps that work when the animal touches, or steps on them, should never be used. They cause great suffering and death to many species of wildlife, birds and pets.

When Peter Rabbit Stops Being Cute:

There are few areas that do not have a native rabbit population and all rabbits are herbivores. Therefore, your plants are at risk. However, their very presence does not mean they will always attack your garden, or that they are a detriment to your environment. I have an interesting patch of weeds in the corner of my yard that stays green and succulent most of the year. My rabbits are very fond of it and will nibble away happily while completely ignoring my good plants!

Rabbits are supremely efficient recyclers. The grasses that they eat are difficult to digest and thus they process their food twice. The soft black pellets that they first produce are consumed a second time, (yuck!) resulting in final small, hard pellets from which most nutrients have been extracted.

Rabbits shelter in abandoned burrows dug by other burrowing animals. They forage at dawn and dusk along the edges of fields and woods. Their excellent vision and hearing are needed to protect them from their many predators, including humans.

If you are having a problem, there are a number of solutions to discourage this critter. Most rabbits are easily kept at bay by one, or more, of the following.

Rabbits are not good climbers or burrowers so a 3-foot high sturdy fence of 1-inch wire discourages them. You can either add a bottom extension underground, which will discourage burrowing animals, as well, or simply bury the lower foot of a three-foot fence underground and have a fence that is two-feet high. If you already have a deer fence add fine wire mesh, such as 1/2" hardware cloth, to the lower part of the deer fence. Rabbits, like mice, can get through amazingly small openings!

Protect individual trees and shrubs by wrapping 1/2-inch wire mesh around the trunk. Keep lawns around gardens and orchards mowed and brush cleared away. Rabbits will avoid areas with little cover.

Place one-liter, uncapped, soda bottles with bottoms cut out over seedlings to protect them.

If rabbits are eating your tulip bulbs, place cut rosebush branches above where bulbs are planted. The more thorns the better. You can also lay down gopher, or chicken, wire.

If the plants you wish to protect are ornamental and not food crops. **Ropel** can be sprayed on them to give them a bitter taste but does not harm wildlife.

Rabbits are sensitive to odors. Lavender or a homemade mixture consisting of a cup of chopped fresh mint leaves pureed in a blender with a head of garlic and a little water will repel rabbits.

Decreasing Tree Squirrel Problems:

The goal here is just keeping them under control so you can enjoy the amazing, fascinating, entertaining, smart, clever, playful, curious, and human-like squirrels commonly found in our neighborhoods. A closer look at squirrels reveals that each squirrel has its own personality. Some are outgoing, some shy, and some bold. With a little effort and flexibility on your part, squirrels may no longer be considered a pest.

Tree squirrels are not the same as the previously mentioned ground squirrel. Even though ground squirrels can climb, trees are not their natural habitat. If you have tree squirrels you probably have, you guessed it, trees. If the trees have nuts, pinecones or fruit that squirrels like, squirrels will be especially attracted. The easiest way to deal with squirrels is to work out a way to live harmoniously with them. Even if you use deterrents, expect that they will eat some of the foods that you might grow on or near their trees. Squirrels are comparatively harmless, and their behavior can fascinate both children and adults. If the squirrels inhabiting the trees were somehow to disappear, there would soon be other squirrels attracted to the trees. Squirrels have an important place in neighborhood ecosystems.

Squirrels are active only during the day. If unwanted activity is occurring at night, your visitor is another species of animal. Squirrels rarely do significant damage to plants and trees, actually preferring food that humans do not eat, such as acorns. They may eat some buds, fruits and bulbs in the spring and instinctively bury nuts in the fall. Do you have an oak or nut tree? Why not share it with the squirrels? Nuts, pinecones and acorns are favorite foods of squirrels, and if you have these trees you can enjoy watching the antics of squirrels in your own yard.

Remember that squirrels and other wildlife must find all their food in nature. There are no supermarkets for wildlife. Plus, it is unlikely that you will have such an invasion that the squirrels will make a significant dent in your tree's bounty. Anyone living around cone bearing firs and pines know that the squirrels prefer the seed-filled cones. The only danger would be when the squirrels toss their ravaged cones. You could be under said squirrel and get an unwelcomed conk on the head.

Controlling squirrel populations is the first step. If people are not feeding squirrels, the natural habitat in your neighborhood will support only a given number of squirrels. The ecological balance will be maintained naturally.

Squirrels are instinctively attracted to trees for their very survival, for much of their food, and for nesting. Deterring them from specific trees is an ongoing challenge. Spraying squirrels with water from a hose may work for a while. Eventually, the squirrels will run away when they see you pick up the hose or even move toward it. Therefore, this may be more of waste of water than a deterrent. Instead, tie a 2-foot band of sheet metal around the trunk of the tree about 6 feet off the ground. Make sure that there are no nearby launching sites from which they can jump to the tree.

Squirrels love to bury nuts, etc. for storage. Unfortunately, they are very short memories. Therefore, any time they note freshly dug, soft soil, they will dig around to see if there are buried treasures. This means that even if they find something inedible they will uproot it in the process. Here's an easy solution. Chicken wire is unobtrusive and bendable and can solve many squirrel issues. Place a flat layer of ordinary chicken, or gopher, wire over plants and on the ground's surface where squirrels are digging to bury, or find food. A few stones or bricks around the edges of the wire should hold it in place.

The openings in the wire will be big enough for plants to grow through. Wherever unwanted squirrel digging, or gnawing, is discovered, a piece of chicken wire can be used, even on the top of a gate or over roof shingles.

Smooth rocks placed around plants in the ground or in pots look attractive and will deter squirrels from burying their treasures in that location. Frequently, when you see squirrels digging up your newly planted bulbs, they are not necessarily going to eat them. They are just looking to see if they are edible. Unfortunately, we have yet to be able to train a squirrel to replant them! As soon as your bulbs are planted, lay down piece of chicken wire and your problem is solved.

Again, avoid bird netting. It is notorious for trapping and entangling visitors such as skunks, raccoons, and opossums, causing them great distress. Imagine how challenging it would be to free a skunk or raccoon that becomes trapped under the netting. Freeing a squirrel is equally challenging!

Grate Irish Spring soap with a cheese grater, and sprinkle it lightly through your garden. Mix a small bottle of hot sauce, a teaspoon of dish soap, and a gallon of water and spray the mixture onto ornamental plants that humans do not eat. After a rain the hot sauce must be reapplied. **Ropel** is a commercial animal repellent that can be used <u>on inedible plants.</u> It makes them taste very bitter to animals.

Many baby squirrels are victims of ill-timed tree trimming. In the Northern Hemisphere, trim most trees in late November, December, and early January when squirrels and most birds are not nesting, not during spring, summer, and early fall, when squirrels and birds are having young. In the Southern Hemisphere, trim trees in months when squirrels and birds are not nesting. If you absolutely must trim a tree during squirrel and bird nesting season, please examine the tree carefully to make sure that you avoid squirrel nests and bird nests. Be sure to leave plenty of foliage around the nests so that the young squirrels and birds will not be exposed to predators and the hot sun. Please share this information with your gardener. Especially during nesting season squirrels dart back and forth across streets. Remember, if a squirrel mother is killed, her babies will starve to death or be eaten by predators.

When crossing the road, squirrels instinct is to dart back and forth to elude predators, which include vehicles. Squirrels can change direction suddenly and dart back into traffic. If you spot a squirrel in or near the road, reduce speed so that you can easily and quickly stop.

Squirrel mothers seek warm, dry places for their nests, sometimes other than trees. They may enlarge openings in roofs to find a suitable place, unfortunately causing some damage to your home. It is best to let the mother squirrel raise her babies before trying to chase them all out. When the babies are teenagers (at about 13 weeks), you can repel the squirrel family by playing a radio loudly or banging on the bottom of a metal pot. The mother squirrel may decide to transfer her babies to another nest, as she usually has a backup elsewhere. This process may take 3-5 days. Never separate a mother squirrel from her babies, and give her time to relocate them. To be sure the squirrel family has left, listen and watch for 5-6 days before sealing the access holes where they entered in your attic and foundation areas.

You may want to place a Havahart trap (humane, live trap) in the sealed area for a week or two to ensure that no other squirrels remain inside. Check it daily, and release any trapped squirrels outdoors on your property during the day.

Install a cap on your chimney. Young squirrels are adventurous and sometimes fall into an uncapped chimney. At other times, adult squirrels seeking shelter may try to nest in the chimney.

There are several styles of bird feeders that supposedly deter squirrels. Nevertheless, squirrels usually figure out how to reach the seed. Feeders must be positioned at least 10 feet from any launching point. One simple strategy is to place a length of plastic tubing around the wire from which the bird feeder is suspended. The tube will spin when the squirrel tries to walk on it.

It is important to allow squirrels, birds, and other wild animals to find their own food in nature. Therefore, you may want to consider removing the bird feeders and having birdbaths instead. Birds need fresh, clean water all year long. Bird feeders can present problems. Spilled birdseed from a feeder can attract rats and other wild creatures. Sick birds that use feeders can spread diseases. Clusters of birds at bird feeders can attract hawks that prey upon the birds as they eat. Birdbaths that are cleaned and refilled regularly with fresh water provide a much healthier attraction for birds throughout the entire year.

A Special Section on Native Plants:

Using native plants is a good idea no matter where you live. It's good for the soil, good for the gardener and good for the ecology. Our environment loses more and more support for our wildlife every year. This is due to expansion of human habitats, replacing soil surfaces with pavements, roads, buildings etc. As any gardener knows, each and every plant and creature on our planet is tied in numerous ways to every other plant and creature. By using native plants we still can have beauty and also save water and other resources. For example, caterpillars and bees are not only important, they are essential to our survival. However, each species requires plants that are NATIVE to their location. Milk weed plants that give monarch butterflies a place to lay their eggs, and butterfly bushes providing nourishment, must be the right kind, or they can be more a danger than a benefit. In colder climates the Monarch must head south before the winter sets in. If, however, the gardener's plants were originally native to warmer climes, they may bloom longer and encourage the Monarch to stay until it is too late for them to escape the cold.

There is no longer time to waste. Mankind needs to replace the lost natural resources by planting natives in our yards and gardens. There is no longer enough wild land to support birds, bees, insects, etc. who depend on them.

Information you need to be successful in your native plant garden: Summer is the most difficult time to plant successfully. Early fall through early spring are the best times.

The following information is courtesy of one of Southern California's premium native plant nurseries, the Tree of Life in San Juan Capistrano.

Establishing your container-grown native plants:

Watering : It is important that the root ball does not dry out during the first two, or three, months. Irrigate once a week, being careful to avoid oversoaking the surrounding soil. After two months, water deeply. However, do not let the ground to remain soggy. Natives need deep moisture and cool roots to find oxygen. Usually one deep watering every two or three weeks in the summer and fall, once the plants are established. Water less often in the spring and little, if any, watering should be required in the winter. Avoid overhead watering on hot summer days.

Use organic mulch in the late spring and fall to help retain water, cool the roots, discourage weeds and strengthen the plants.

You can fertilize in the cooler seasons (Oct-May) with all-purpose plant foods. Use about half of the recommended amount for ornamentals.

Pruning should be done to control the growth of the plant and to dead-head. Remove dead wood. Generally speaking, thin the plants in early summer and mulch. Start feeding in the fall and mulch again. Native plants need love too and should reward you by attracting beautiful birds and butterflies to your yard.

Garden Types:

Protected Ground Level:

An advantage to a ground level, enclosed garden, is that it can be large. It can also be divided into sections that may have different soil types.

The first thing you need to do, once you decide on the size and exterior shape, is to dig down about a foot or two. Place the soil aside and lay down a layer of gopher wire, or hardware cloth. If you use hardware wire be sure you have a deeper layer of dirt since it may impede deeper root growth. Be sure you turn the wire/cloth up at the corners so that all edges will extend above your final ground level. Any overlaps of the screening need to be secured to prevent underground critters from wiggling between the upper and lower levels of the overlap.

You can now build the upper frame work, the depth of the soil simply being determined by the height of your enclosure. By inserting divider walls within the framework, you can create different levels of soil and types. You might have one section with only one foot of soil for plants with very shallow roots, such as lettuces and herbs and another section with a much deeper level for root crops like beets and carrots. One soil may be sandier and the other richer, depending on what you are growing.

The dividers should be solid to keep the plants and soils from crossing over.   Now, mix your choice of garden soils, compost, etc. with the original soil you dug out and fill in. Don't make most of soil levels way below the height of the enclosure as this will make it difficult to lean over and reach the soil for weeding etc. Don't fill all the way to the top or you could lose valuable soil and moisture when you water.

I would recommend that the uprights used in your frame extend a couple of feet above the frame to which you can tack gopher wire in order to surround the garden. One side of this fencing should be framed so it will work as a gate to give you easy access to your garden. Note: When fencing with wire, make it a little loose to create a wiggle factor. If a fence is real sturdy, a raccoon, or possum, can climb and clear it easily. However they don't like to climb something that feels unstable. If you have this problem, as well as deer in your garden, you may also want to create a framed screen to place across the top. This all sounds labor intensive, but is a long-term and satisfactory answer to many of your concerns.

Container Type Gardens:

Despite popular opinion, container gardens are not limited to a few potted plants on your porch. With a little imagination and not much money, you can grow a large variety of flowers and veggies in a number of protective containers, or forms of containment. There are also many benefits to these options, especially for mountain, or desert, gardeners.

First, if done right, they are terrific water savers. Any water you use is going directly to the plants and not being wasted on surrounding non-productive ground.

You will be able to keep your garden weed free with minimal labor.

You can save money on amendments and fertilizers because you're not 'broadcasting' the materials over a large area. Also it is so much more efficient to amend each container as required by the plant being grown there.

They also restrict certain spreading plants from invading other areas of your garden.

Depending on which type of containers you use, you may be able to move your plants to different locations to either take advantage of more or less sun, as required, to a protected area in cases of unusually hot, or cold weather, or to plant earlier than usual by moving your plants indoors (i.e. a garage) at night, and into the sunlight during the day.

Contained gardens can guarantee NO loss to underground varmints!

Let's talk about the various styles of containment from which you can choose, the simplest being the common flowerpot. The most complex being a raised garden.

Above Ground Flower Pots:

Above ground pots come in numerous sizes, are moveable and can grow many flowers, herbs and vegetables, depending on their required soil depth. Make sure they have good drainage holes and, preferably, sit in a dish that will hold the drained water so that the plant(s) can absorb the water from the roots up, as needed.

One drawback to <u>above ground pots</u> is that they are more susceptible to outside temperatures. They will dry out quickly in hot weather, thereby requiring more watering. Cold weather can cool the soil too much and damage the root systems. This is when their mobility is an advantage. For example, if your weather report says you are going to get a 'cold snap', let's say down to 20 degree, you can move your plants into a shed, or garage. It will still be cold in there, but probably 10 to 15 degrees warmer than the outside temperature.

In Ground Containers:

    Taking this option to the next level is one of my favorite ways to garden in the mountains. Using 5 to 18 gallon containers, I drill holes in the bottom and a few more about three inches up on the sides. Then I put in a shallow layer of medium gravel. Now, wherever you decide is the best place to plant, dig a hole to a depth within an inch or so of the top of the container. Once the container is placed in the ground, fill-in the exterior dirt in around it and fill the container with the soil of your choice. If the native soil is fairly weed free and not clay feel free to mix some in with the new soil. This will increase the volume without having to spend as much on the new soil. Select the container size based on the depth needed for a good root system.

I find that even large tomato plants can grow very well in a 15 to 18 gallon container. In the spring you can find big, 18 gallon rubber tote buckets in most discount stores for less than $10 each and buried in the ground, they will last for several years. Be sure they have a fairly heavy gauge plastic that is more difficult for gophers to chew. No gopher will be able to reach the main roots, and you can add fences or covers of gopher wire around the tops to discourage above ground munchers. Burying the containers will allow the soil to retain water longer and it will stay warmer when it's cold.

This is also a good way to grow more when your sunny areas are widely disbursed. Don't skimp on the number of buckets. If you try to plant too much in each bucket, your plants may be stunted or even die from the over-crowding. After the first season, you'll have a better idea of which buckets could have supported more plants.

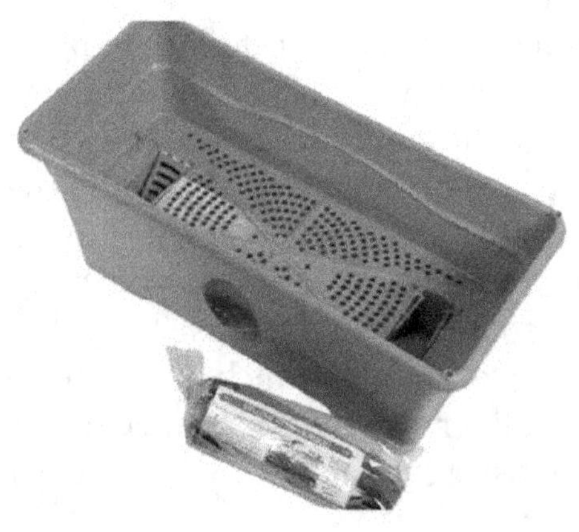

Another wonderful container known as a tomato box, or grow box, solves three potential problems. Gopher invasions, soil value control and watering. These containers do not have to be buried to do their jobs. They are usually used for tomatoes, but can be used for any plant that normally bears flowers or fruit above ground level.

They are trough shaped and have a reservoir in the bottom and an area for soil above that. There is usually a drain at the top of the reservoir to allow excess water to drain, for example during a heavy rain. There is also a hole, or spout at the top so that water may be added as needed without wetting the plants themselves.

The many benefits are that the water in the reservoir doesn't evaporate so you don't need to water as often. It's a convenient place to pour small amounts of left over water, such as half-finished glasses of water, cooking water etc. so that none of it goes to waste. The roots of the plant simply absorb the water as needed. Gophers cannot get to the roots at all. The box can be placed on the ground, or on a table, which will prevent rabbit and ground squirrel attacks too. They can be moved, if needed, to optimize the amount of sunlight required. (Once filled and watered they will be VERY heavy.)

Each box will support two good sized tomato plants. I would still recommend using a tomato cage, or some other form of support, since tomato plants get top-heavy as their fruits grows and ripens.

Raised Gardens:

Whether your raised garden is almost ground level, or three feet off the ground, it can accomplish several goals. It protects against animals destroying the plants, makes it easier to feed and water, can make it easier on the back when weeding, pruning or harvesting.

Waist high frames for your gardens are extremely convenient. Often not mentioned when designing, or buying, such a planter is to consider adding wheels! This mobility will let you move plants into protected or sunny areas as needed and to start plants earlier by being able to protect them on cold nights while they are still tender, without having to have a greenhouse.

One drawback is that they are small. However, have several of them and you can grow quite a bit. They can also be as deep or shallow as you need. Protect the bottom of above ground wood frames so that water doesn't collect and rot the wood. A great way to do that is to attach one, or more fairly shallow pan(s), to the underside of the frame, being sure the drain holes in the frame base, are above the pan(s). A layer of gravel below the soil will help too. Check for designs and blueprints on line. There is a wonderful assortment to fit almost any need. With this option you will not need any gopher wire on the bottom and you can create an upper frame work, using thin PVC pipe, to protect from climbing and flying critters, or to add shade if needed. (Think of how the top of a Conestoga wagon is designed.)

Important! If your raised garden actually rests on the ground, you need to protect it from gophers coming up from below.. About 1 inch in from the perimeter, dig down about 4 to 6 inches. Now, place a layer of gopher wire at the bottom and bring it over and beyond the outside of the box. You can now refill the box with the dirt you dug and any other garden soil you wish.

One last bit of advice. Once winter comes, you may forget where and what you planted; what did, or did not, do well; challenges you discovered and what you wish you had, or hadn't planted. Keep a little notebook handy as the growing season progresses and make notes. You will be so glad you did come next spring! Happy Gardening!

www.ingramcontent.com/pod-product-compliance
Lightning Source LLC
Chambersburg PA
CBHW061519250726

48657CB00005B/1955